★★★
ATLANTA
Braves

JAMES R. ROTHAUS

CREATIVE EDUCATION

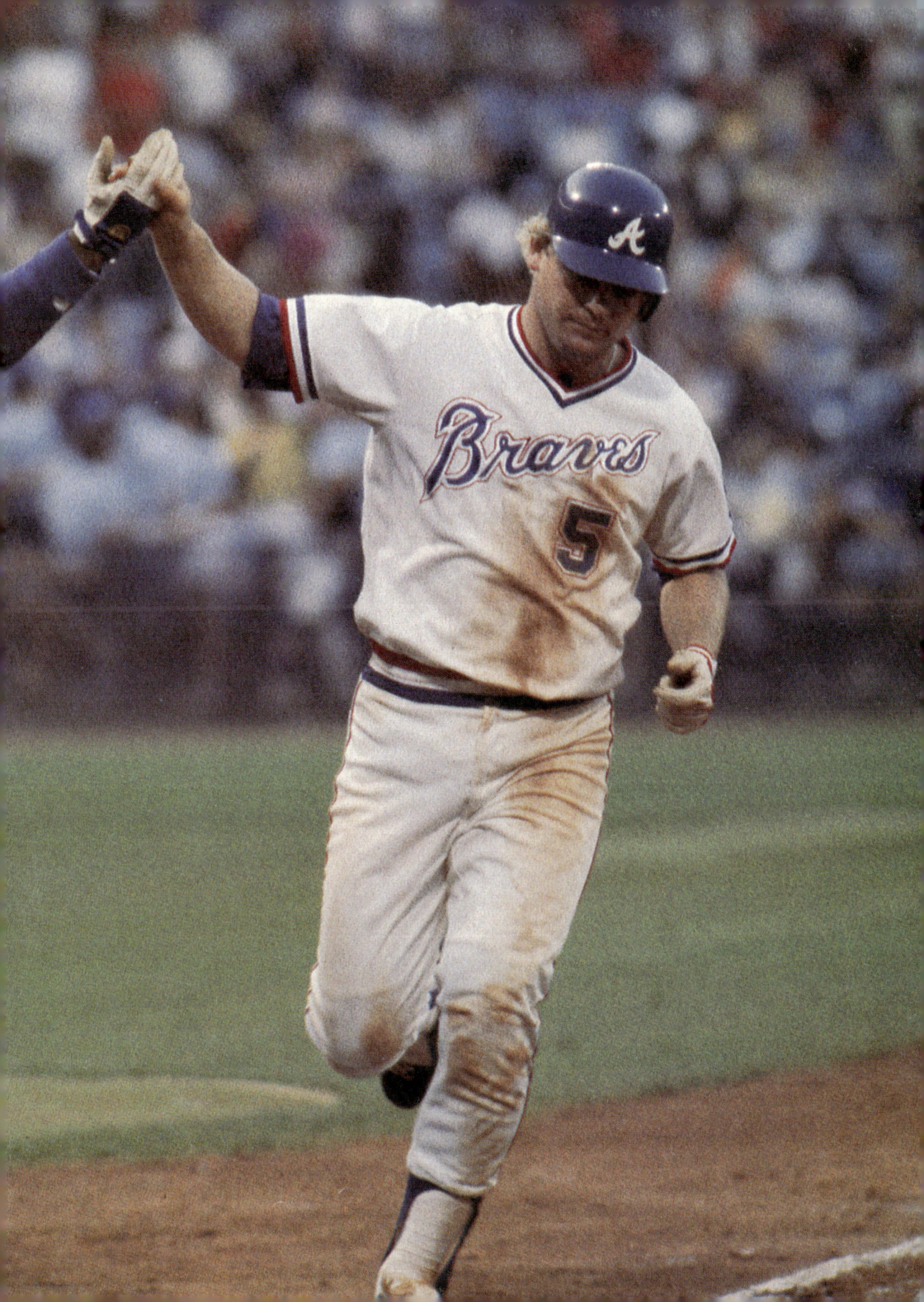
Braves
5

Library of Congress Cataloging-in-Publication Data

Rothaus, James.
　Atlanta Braves.

　　1. Atlanta Braves (Baseball team) — History.　I. Title.
GV875.A8R68　1987　　796.357'64'09758231　　87-20167
ISBN 0-88682-128-2

★★★
CONTENTS

Baseball's First Dynasty Of The 1800's 8
The Miracle Braves Of 1914 11
Building Toward The 1948 World Series 15
The Braves' Move From Boston To Milwaukee In 1953 18
Hammerin' Hank Aaron Launches New Era 19
Sparks Fly In The Championship Season Of 1957 .. 24
The Braves Move South To Atlanta 27
Bad Henry Shatters Ruth's Home Run Record 30
The Ted Turner Years 34
Torre's Prediction Comes True In '82 37
World Series Task Force Fizzles 41
Bright New Stars On The Horizon 45

COVER PHOTO
Big Chief! Dale Murphy is one of the N.L.'s toughest competitors, and a pillar of power for the Braves of the late 1980's.

PHOTO SPREAD (PAGE 2/3)
Mr. Inspiration! Bob Horner high-fives Watson in the on-deck circle. (1986)

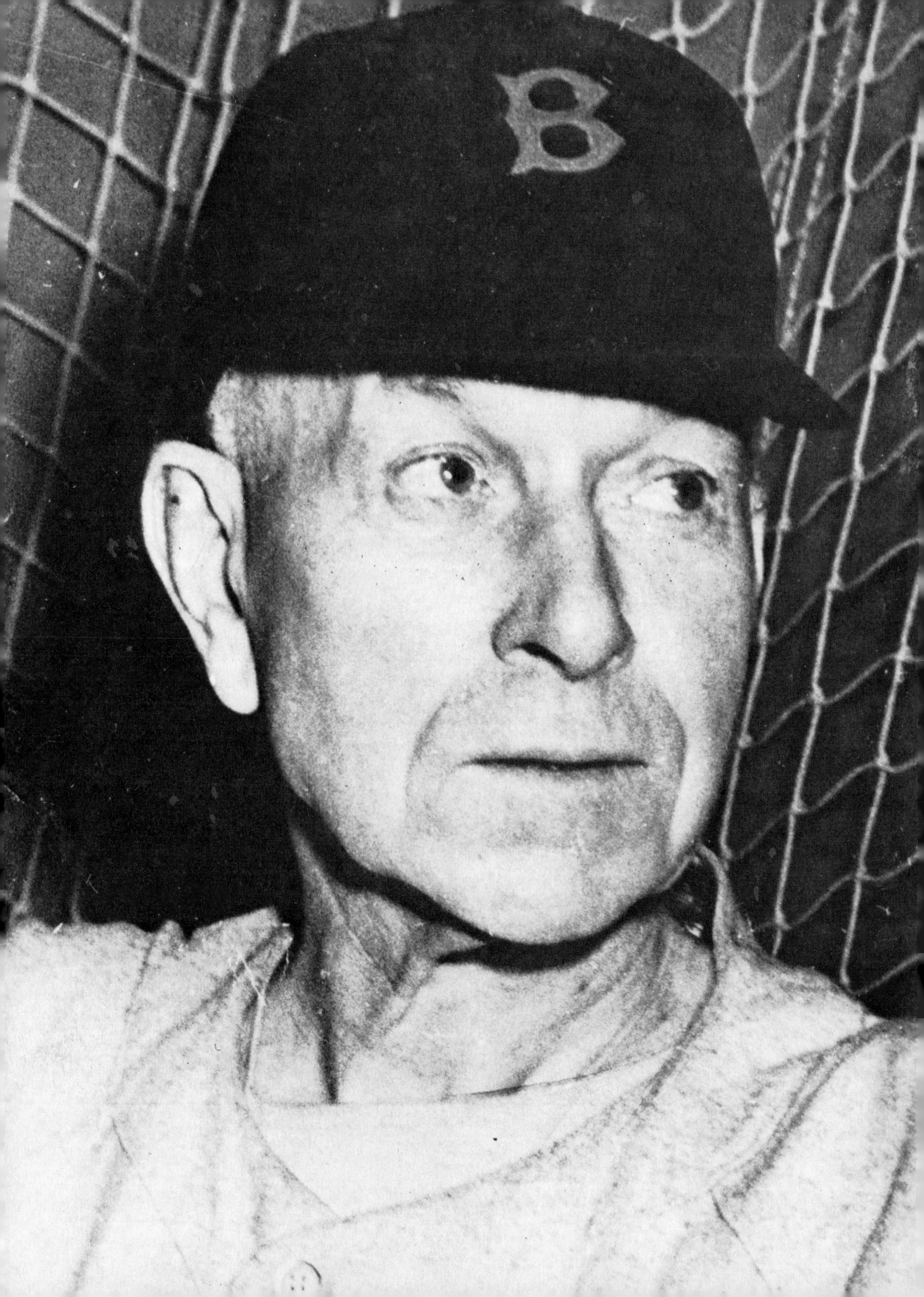

The people of Boston, Massachusetts, were mad! The year was 1876, and most of the country was celebrating the 100th anniversary of the United States. But in Boston, America's "cradle of liberty," people were thinking more about baseball.

You see, Boston's baseball team had just won four straight titles in the first professional league — the National Association of Professional Base Ball Players. The team was so powerful that the league's executives feared no one else would ever win the championship. They also worried about rumors of cheating and gambling. So they simply shut down the league. That made the people of Boston mad. But they didn't give up. They had learned not to give up one century earlier when they were fighting for their country's independence.

The Boston team regrouped and entered the new National League. The Braves were born.

Since then, the Braves have done a lot of moving around. The team moved to Milwaukee, Wisconsin in 1953, where they won another World Championship. And in 1966, they moved again to Atlanta, Georgia.

That's where the Braves can be found today. And, after more than 100 years, the Atlanta Braves still have the same determination as their pioneer founders.

Since 1876, more than 54 million people have cheered the Braves through to a dozen National League pennants.

In certain ways, the Braves have been like most other baseball clubs. Some years, they've challenged for the N.L. pennant. Other years, they've struggled to win even half their games.

But in a few special ways, the Braves are different

1884
Hugh Duffy of the old Boston Braves hits .440 for the season — an all-time Braves high.

PHOTO
Hugh Duffy starred in the 1890's and returned for several "old timers" games throughout the 1900's.

7

1901
The Braves play their very first season in the new National League, finishing fifth under Manager Frank Selee.

PHOTO
The Magician. Dignified George "Tweedy" Stallings took over as manager in 1913 and guided the Braves from nowhere to the World Championship.

from any other club ever.

In 1914, they went from being the worst team in the league to being the World Champions.

When they moved to Milwaukee, they were so popular that they became the first team ever to draw more than 2 million fans in one season.

And the Braves will go down in history as the team of Henry Aaron, who became major league baseball's greatest home run hitter of all time.

Yes, the oldest pro baseball club really has lived up to its heritage over the last hundred years. And it all began with a little bit of anger, back in 1876.

Baseball's First Dynasty Of The 1800's

Baseball was very different in the 1870's. Home runs were rare. The ball was soft, tobacco-stained and not too round. Handlebar moustaches were an important part of the players' uniforms. Catchers still caught barehanded. Many pitchers still pitched underhanded.

But that first Boston team, known then as the Red Stockings, was much better than any other team.

The owner of the team was Ivers Adams. He had gathered together some of the best ball players of that time: George and Harry Wright, Charlie Gould, Roscoe Barnes, Jim O'Rourke and Albert Spalding.

The Red Stockings won National Association titles in 1872, 1873 and 1874. In 1875, four of Boston's stars left to play for the Chicago White Stockings. But Boston still won 71 games, lost only 8, and claimed its fourth straight league crown.

When the N.A. folded and the National League got going in 1876, Boston hardly let up. It won N.L. pen-

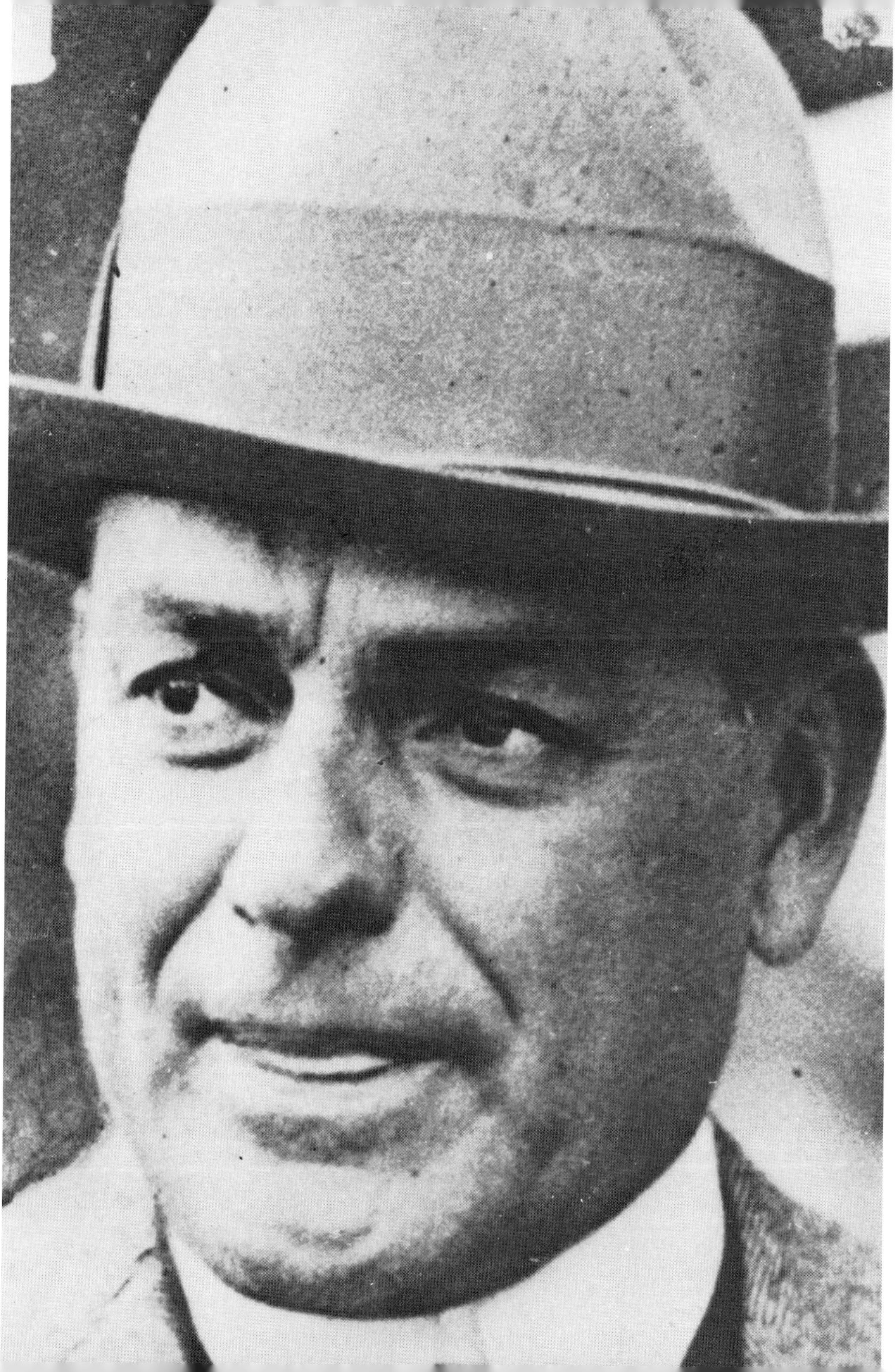

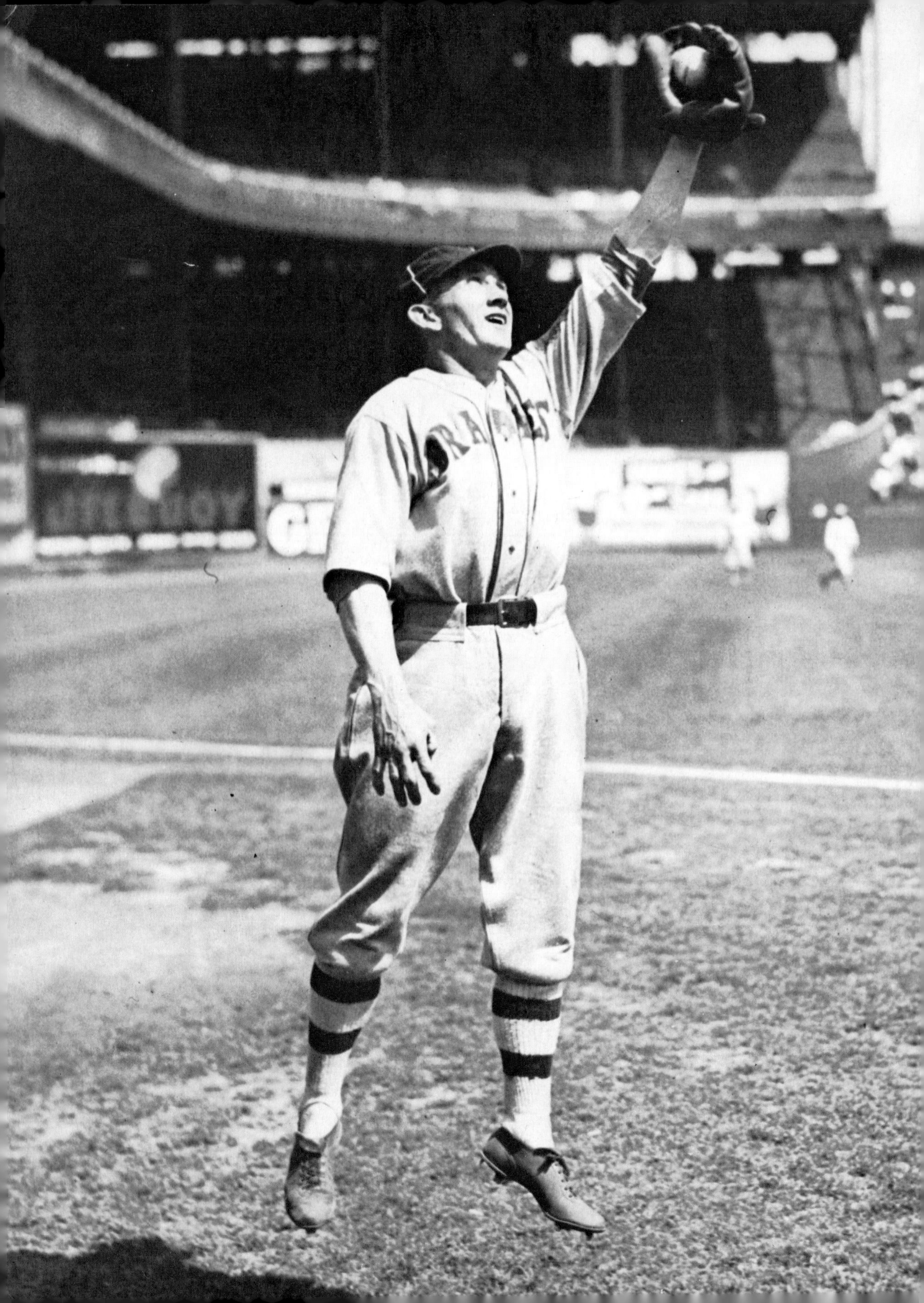

nants 8 more times before the turn of the century.

Before the team finally settled on the nickname Braves, the Boston club was known as the Red Stockings, the Reds, the Red Caps, the Bean-Eaters, the Nationals, the Doves and the Rustlers. In 1901, when the rival American League began, another Boston team took on the nickname Red Sox. But the Braves were the true original team.

The Miracle Braves Of 1914

After the turn of the century, the Braves fell on hard times. From 1900 to 1913, they finished third once, fourth once, fifth two times, sixth twice, seventh three times and eighth five times.

In 1912, the Braves were, once again, the laughingstock of the league. One chilly, gray September day, the owner of the team, James Gaffney, was sitting in the stands as his team was losing to the New York Giants. The Giants would go on to win the N.L. pennant, and the Braves would finish a whopping 52 games behind them.

Beside Gaffney was sitting Boston's new manager, George Tweedy Stallings. Stallings could not believe what he was seeing. He thought the Braves were lazy, careless and not very talented.

Stallings turned to Gaffney and said, "I've been stuck with some terrible teams in my day, but this one beats them all!"

It was just the sort of challenge that Stallings loved. He devoted his heart and soul to rebuilding the Braves. When he was finished, Stallings was known as a magician, and the Boston club was called "The Miracle

1912
To keep a team rally alive, Walter "Rabbit" Maranville leans into a pitch, allowing a fastball to hit him on the head. The automatic walk forces in the winning run.

PHOTO
From 1912 to 1920 the great "Rabbit" Maranville snagged enemy hits from his shortstop slot.

1914
The "Miracle Braves" record the upset of the century by defeating the powerful Philadelphia A's in the first four-game sweep in World Series history.

Braves."

The first thing Stallings did was rework his roster. He started trading players as though they were bubblegum cards. And when he got the players he wanted, he worked them mercilessly.

Stallings was a well-dressed gentleman off the field. He was courteous, well-mannered, charming, even dignified.

But once he put on the manager's uniform, he was a changed man. He would stop at nothing to get the very best out of his players. He shouted at them. He threatened them. He bullied them. But he also had more patience than most of his players had ever seen.

Stallings had a motto: "You can win. You must win. You will win." In 1913, the team finally began to believe in that motto. They jumped from eighth to fifth place.

The year 1914 was a year of change. In Detroit, Henry Ford doubled his workers' pay from $2.50 a day to $5 a day. In Central America, the first ship sailed through the new Panama Canal. In Europe, an archduke was assassinated and World War I began.

In Boston, the Braves were losing again. Walter "Rabbit" Maranville, the Braves' shortstop, was out of the lineup with an illness. So was second baseman Johnny Evers.

Out on the field, nothing seemed to go Boston's way. The team had the worst luck imaginable. They'd lose game after game by one run. The team even lost an exhibition game to a soap company. On July 4, the Braves were in last place, 15 games behind the Giants.

Still, Stallings didn't give up. He believed that he had the ingredients to make a championship team. It was just a matter of time before luck turned their way.

While other teams slept in each morning, Stallings called the Braves to early chalkboard strategy meetings.

Suddenly, as Stallings had predicted, things did begin going Boston's way. The Braves began to play smart, aggressive baseball. They had won just 26 of their first 66 games. They captured 52 of their final 66.

Boston just kept on winning — and the Giants kept on losing. Soon, the entire country was scouring the headlines for word of the Braves. Most baseball fans were tired of hearing about the cocky New York Giants and their pushy manager, John McGraw. And the courageous exploits of the underdog Braves were a welcome relief from news of the war in Europe.

The ragtag Braves had only three good hitters. Only one batter averaged above .300. Boston's outfielders were so weak that Stallings used one trio against right-handed pitchers and another threesome against lefties. But the Braves outhustled, outfought and outsmarted every opponent in the league.

Boston demolished the Giants' 15-game lead in a mere five weeks. By the end of the season, the Braves were a full 10½ games ahead of the team from the Big Apple.

Boston had made it to the World Series!

The Braves' Series opponent was the Philadelphia A's. Philly featured its famed "$100,000 Infield," a group of terrific infielders whose combined income was huge for those days. They also had two future Hall-of-Fame pitchers, Chief Bender and Eddie Plank, and were managed by the crafty Connie Mack.

The A's were 2-to-1 favorites to take the Series, and they got off to the right start by winning the coin flip. That meant the first two games would be played in Philadelphia.

**1914
Second baseman Johnny Evers becomes the first player in Braves history to be named N.L. MVP.**

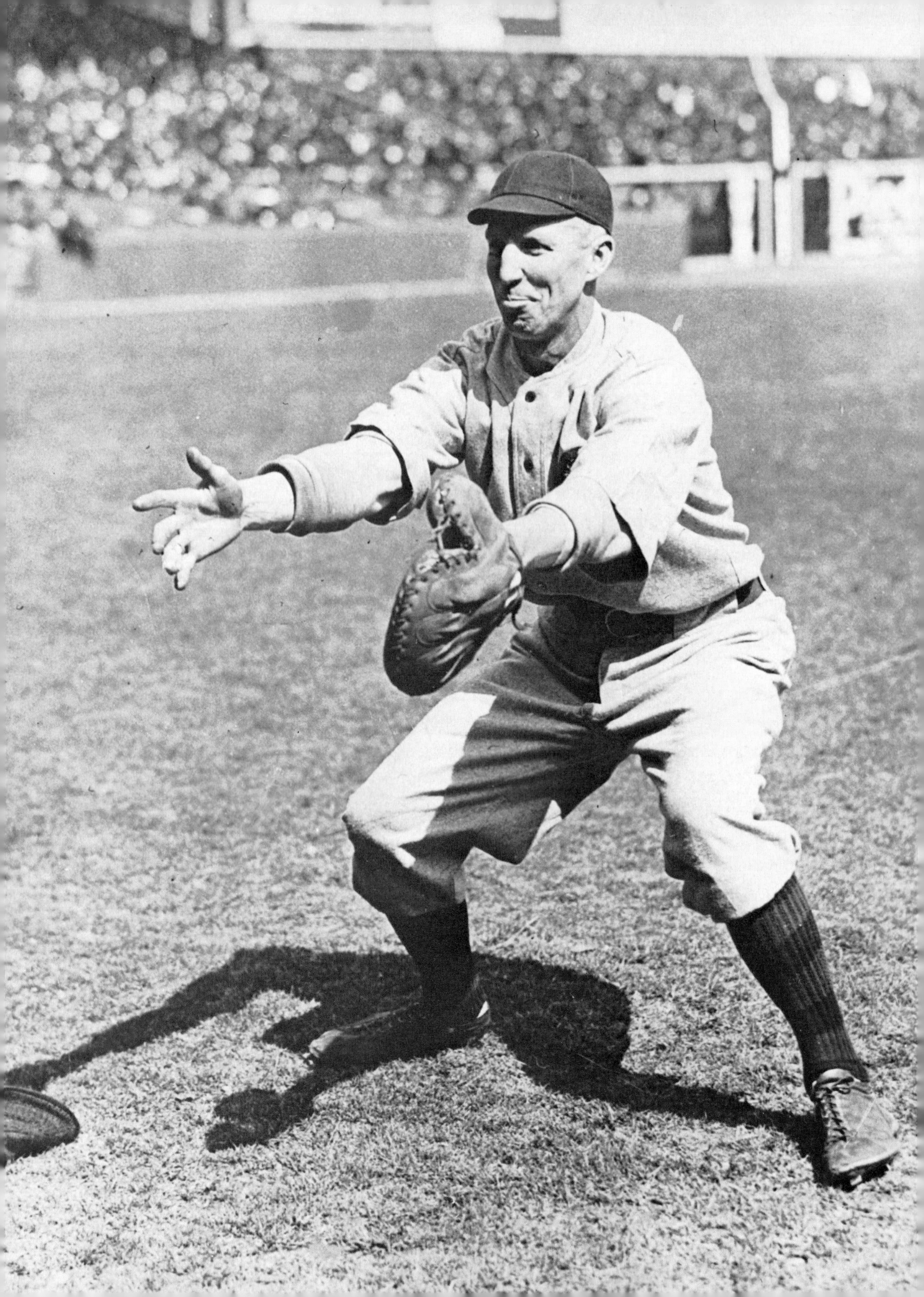

Stallings spent the days before Game One bragging about his team and ridiculing the A's. Stallings told the Braves to ignore the Athletics throughout the Series, unless it was to insult them. By game time, the A's didn't know what to think.

Philadelphia started Chief Bender on the mound in the first game. Bender had won 17 and lost 3 during the season. But the Braves got 8 hits off of him, and Boston won the opener, 7-1.

The Braves won the second game, 1-0, to sweep the A's at home. When they returned to Boston, their fans were chanting, "Four straight, four straight."

They weren't disappointed. Hank Gowdy smashed a home run and two doubles in Game Three, as Boston won in 12 innings, 5-4.

In Game Four, the Braves outscored the A's, 2-1, to capture the first four-game sweep in World Series history. Gowdy, who had hit .243 during the season, batted .545 for the Series.

Thirty-six years later, the country's sportswriters and sportscasters got together to pick the greatest sports upset of the first 50 years of the century. The Miracle Braves of 1914 won, hands down.

Building Toward The 1948 World Series

It would be a long time before the Braves would bring home another World Series crown. They dropped to second place in 1915 and third in 1916. Then, from 1917 through 1946, Boston finished last four times and seventh 11 times. They didn't get as high as third again until 1947.

Stallings stayed with the team until 1920. After that,

1928
Rogers Hornsby sets an all-time Braves slugging average of .632—a record that still stands.

PHOTO
Hank Gowdy, the veteran catcher of the old Boston National Leaguers, was the first major league player to enlist in World War I.

1930
Big Walt Berger bashes a club record 11 homers in a single month.

Boston went through nine more managers through 1947. Two of those were famous for their accomplishments elsewhere: Rogers Hornsby, better known as a player and future Hall-of-Fame member, and Casey Stengel, whose best years as skipper of the Yankees were still to come.

By 1948, however, Boston had again put together a championship team. Everything was being modernized after World War II, and even Braves Field got some of those newfangled lights that let the teams play baseball at night.

Billy Southworth was the Braves' manager. He had two great pitchers, right-hander Johnny Sain and lefty Warren Spahn. But the Braves didn't have much depth behind those two pitchers, so Southworth used them a lot. The saying around Boston about the Braves' pitching rotation was, "Spahn, Sain, then pray for rain."

The Braves didn't really need to do much praying in 1948. Sain won 23 games and lost 15. Boston got five players into the All-Star game—third baseman Bob Elliott, outfielder Tommy Holmes, catcher Phil Masi, starting pitcher Sain and second base Eddie Stankey.

Boston won 91 games, lost 62, and finished 6½ games ahead of the Cardinals to win their first N.L. pennant in 34 years. On to the World Series!

The 1948 Series pitted the Braves against the Cleveland Indians. Boston shelled Cleveland's famous fastballer, Bob Feller, to win two games in the Series. Sain and Spahn got those victories. But Bob Lemon won two games of his own for the Indians. Another Cleveland pitcher, Gene Bearden, won a third and pitched almost 11 Series innings without allowing a run. The Braves lost the World Championship, four games to two.

PHOTO
The amazing Warren Spahn rears up to fire one, early in the fourth game of the '58 Series against the Yanks. As usual, Spahn got the victory.

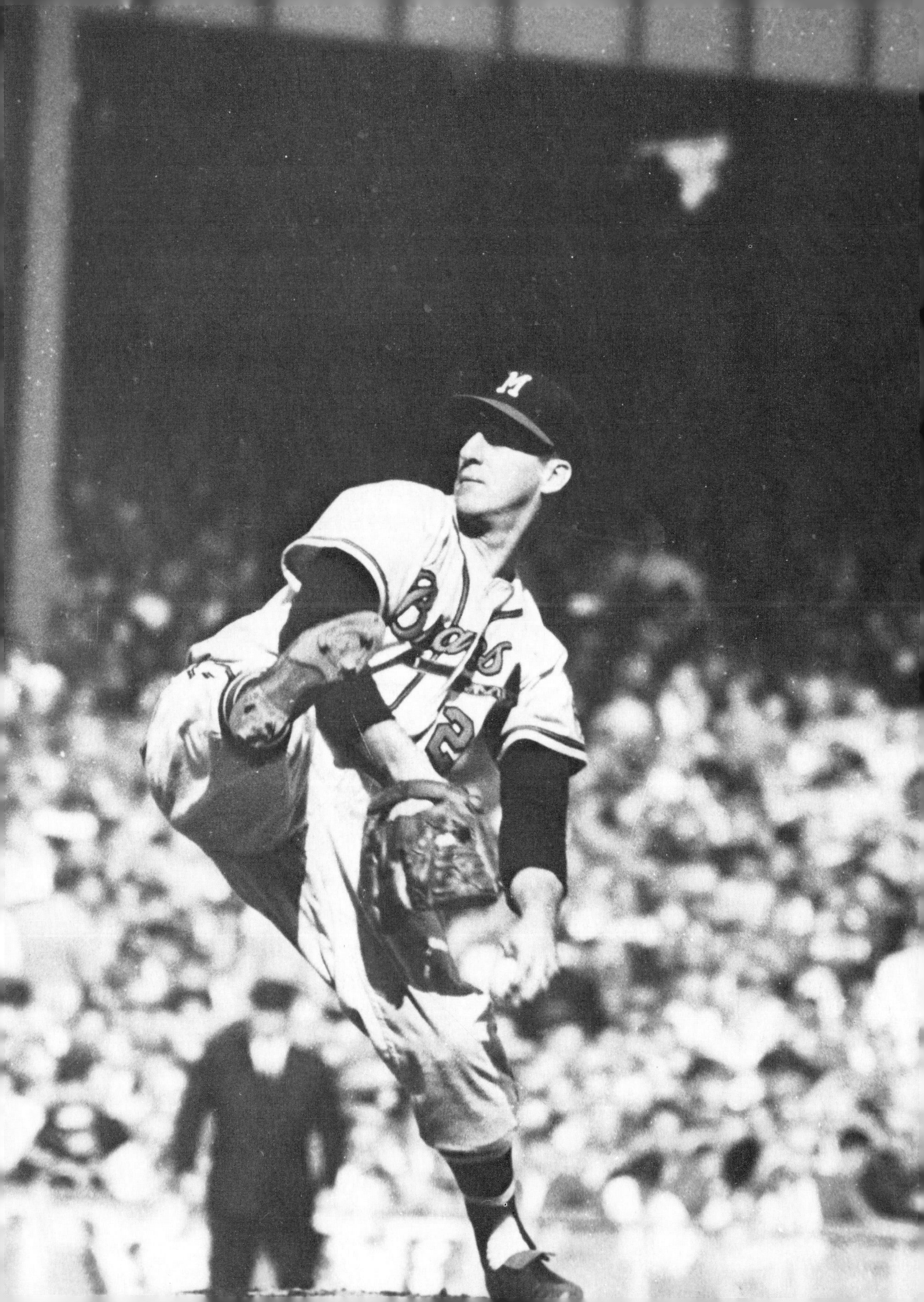

1936-40
The club is known as the Boston Bees. (In 1941, the name is changed back to the Braves for good.)

The Braves' Move From Boston To Milwaukee In 1953

Again, as in 1914, the Braves fell after their pennant winning season. Boston was fourth in 1949, in 1950 and again in 1951. In 1952, the Braves dropped to that familiar seventh place.

Even more worrisome than Boston's record, though, was its attendance. More than one million fans watched the team in 1949. By 1952, however, that number had dropped below 300,000. That spelled disaster for the team. It lost $600,000 in 1952.

Braves' owner Loui Perini also owned the Milwaukee team in the American Association. He knew how much Milwaukee wanted a major league team. He convinced the owners of the other seven N.L. clubs to approve the move, and the Boston Braves became the Milwaukee Braves.

Milwaukee couldn't have been happier, and it let the players know it. Braves in Milwaukee were treated like kings. They were showered with gifts and free services. An automobile dealer loaned each player a new car every year. Another company did all the players' laundry and dry cleaning, free of charge. Free gas. Free food. Free clothes. You name it, the Braves got it. They even had a new ball park, Milwaukee County Stadium.

The Braves wasted no time showing their appreciation to the citizens of Milwaukee. The ink had hardly dried in the record books from their seventh-place 1952 finish, when the Braves rebounded for second in 1953.

Charlie Grimm was the manager, and he had some very special players to manage, including legendary pitchers Warren Spahn and Lew Burdette. Spahn, a future Hall-of-Famer, would eventually rack up more games than any left-handed pitcher in history. Burdette was a tall, smiling righthander. Opposing batters believed that Lew smiled because he threw a mean spitball.

Then there was first baseman Joe Adcock, who batted .285 in '53; second baseman Jack Dittmer (.266); shortstop Johnny Logan (.273) and catcher Del Crandall (.272).

Next came third baseman Eddie Mathews (.302). He led the N.L. in 1953 with 47 home runs, and would also be elected to the Hall of Fame. Outfielders Andy Pafko (.297); Bill Bruton (the league-leader with 26 stolen bases); and Sid Gordon (.274).

This core was the beginning of a club that would, over a period of eight years, finish first twice, second five times and third once. But no single player would turn out to be more valuable than a skinny rookie who showed up for the 1954 spring training camp. His name was Henry Aaron.

**1945
Tommy Holmes scores a record 125 runs in a single season.**

"Hammerin'" Hank Aaron Launches New Era

Henry Louis Aaron was born on February 5, 1934, in Mobile, Alabama. Young Henry at first wanted to be an airplane pilot. He was crushed when his father told him, "Forget it, son. There are no black airline pilots."

There hadn't been any black major league baseball players, either. Until 1947, that is. That's when Jackie Robinson broke baseball's color line and became a Brooklyn Dodger.

Aaron also liked baseball. With Robinson as his idol,

**1950
Sidney Gordon launches 4 grand slams in a single season.**

Henry changed his plans and decided to become a professional ball player.

At the age of 15, Aaron went to a Dodgers tryout in Mobile, but he didn't even get a chance to show his skills. He was so timid that the older, bigger players shoved him out of the way.

But Aaron did have talent. He had a fluid grace that made hitting and fielding look easy. He was 5-foot-11 and weighed only 140 pounds. He was a smart, all-around ball player. And he had those wrists. The wrists. If there was one superhuman quality in Aaron, it was his wrists. They were huge—eight inches around, as big as those of Muhammad Ali, the boxer. Those wrists were strong. They were quick. And they were the secret of snapping a bat with tremendous speed.

Aaron was 17 when he got an offer to play each Sunday for Mobile's semi-pro club. "I'll have to ask Mama," Henry said. He did, and Mrs. Aaron agreed, but only after Henry promised that he'd still go to church each Sunday before leaving for the game. He earned between $3 and $10 each game.

The next year, Aaron joined a barnstorming team, the Indianapolis Clowns of the old Negro League. He was paid $200 a month. His .467 average caught plenty of scouts' eyes, and Aaron was signed by the Braves in 1952.

One and a half years in the minor leagues was all Aaron needed to convince the Braves that he was a major league player. When spring of 1954 arrived, Aaron was in the Braves' training camp, waiting for a chance to prove himself.

One day during that spring training, Aaron was standing under the bleachers, drinking a soda pop. He'd been

**PHOTO
If you had played against the 1957 Braves, you'd have faced this man, Big Lew Burdette, who pitched two straight World Series shutouts.**

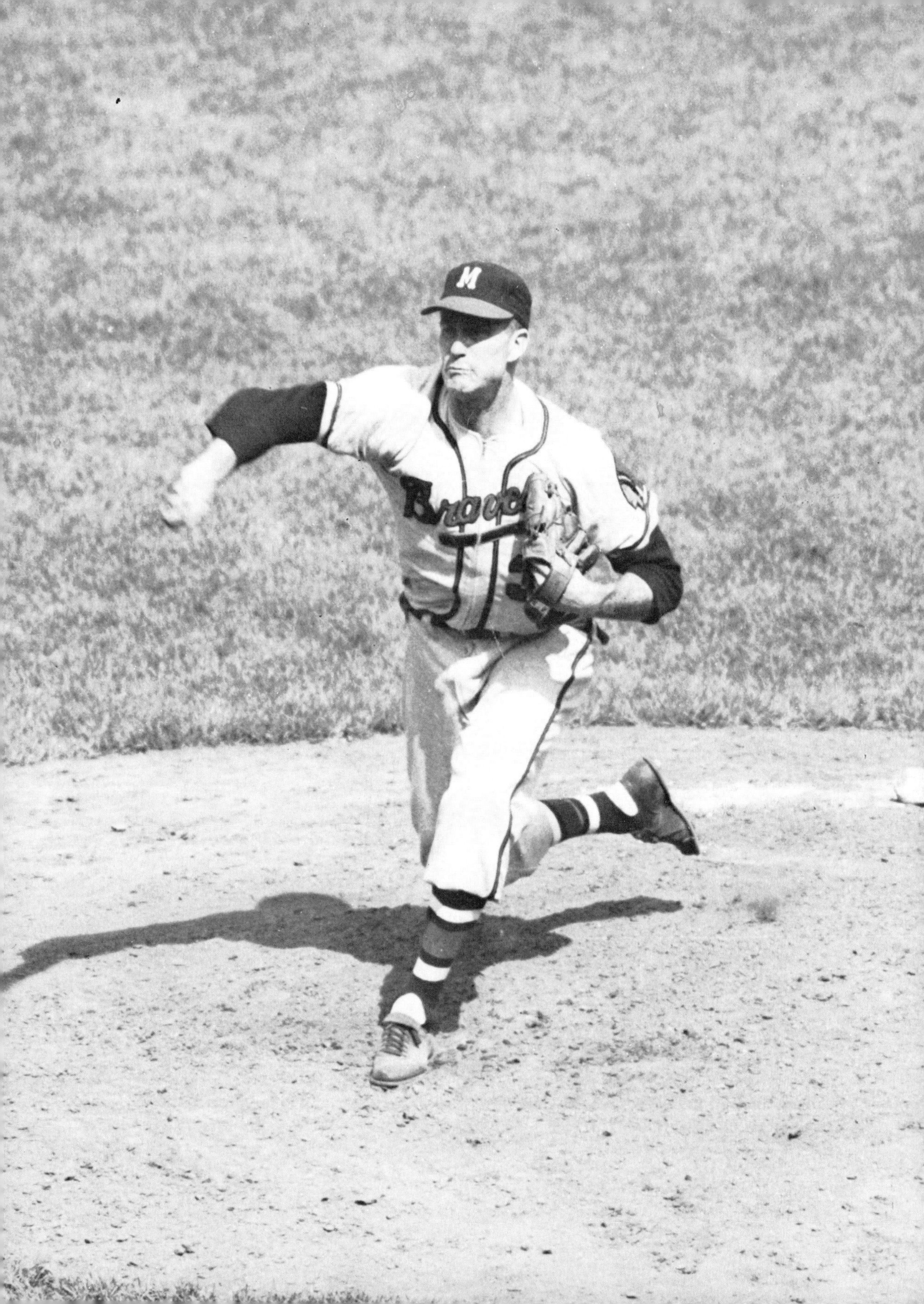

1953
The Braves move from Boston to Milwaukee, becoming the first N.L. club since 1900 to shift locations.

pinch-hitting during an exhibition game, and was waiting for his next turn at bat.

Suddenly, he heard a faint crack, followed by a moan. Bobby Thomson, the Braves' new rightfielder, had broken his ankle sliding into base. Everyone groaned. Thomson was supposed to really help Milwaukee that year, both in the field and at the plate.

Aaron was as concerned as anyone over Thomson's ankle. He was also as surprised as anyone when manager Charlie Grimm threw Aaron his mitt and told him to take over in right field.

This was Henry's big chance, and he made the most of it. That year, he batted .280 and hit 13 home runs, even though he, too, broke an ankle late in the season.

Aaron upped his average to .314 in 1955. Over the next 20 seasons with the Braves, he would hit .300 or better 14 times!

Pitchers would eventually call Aaron "Bad Henry." They gave him that nickname because sometimes Aaron looked downright bored going to the plate. But any pitcher who let up, just a little bit, would see their next pitch go sailing out of the ball park.

Of course, Aaron alone wasn't enough to make the other teams just give the Braves the National League pennant. For Aaron's first few years with the club, Milwaukee had to take a back seat to the accomplishments of the Brooklyn Dodgers.

Milwaukee finished second in 1953. In 1954, Aaron's rookie year, they finished third.

In 1955, Aaron hit .314, got 189 hits, 27 homers and batted in 106 runs. The Braves moved back up to second.

In 1956, the Braves lost the pennant on the last day of

**PHOTO
Hammerin' Hank!
Bad Henry Aaron broke Babe Ruth's home run record on April 8, 1974, in Atlanta Stadium.**

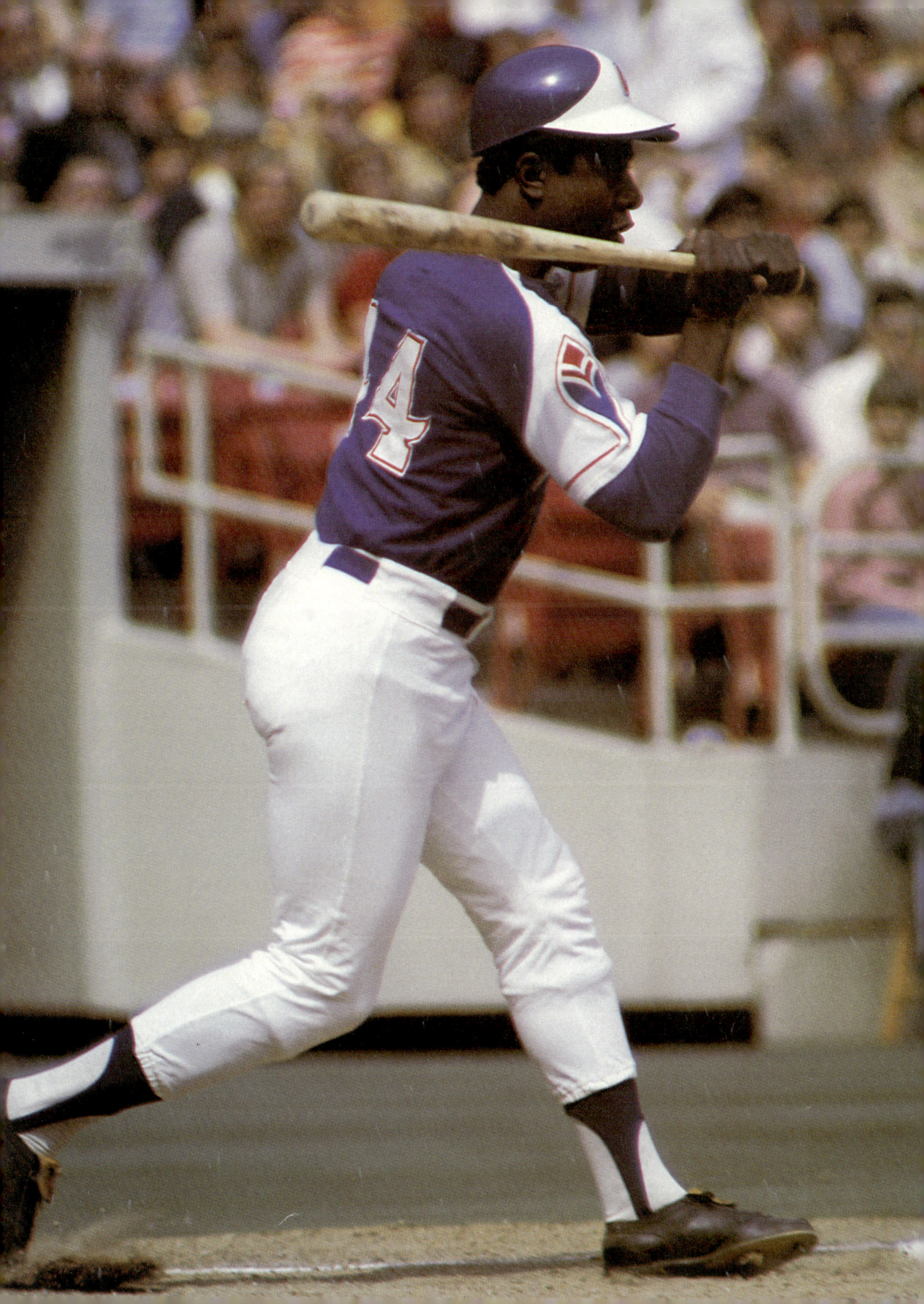

1954
Rookie Henry Aaron hits 13 homers in his first season with the Milwaukee Braves.

the season and again had to settle for second place.

Sparks Fly In
The Championship Season Of 1957

In 1957, everything fell into place.

Milwaukee traded for a new second baseman, Red Schoendienst. Red solidified the Braves' infield, and was a fine hitter.

By then, Aaron had moved to the cleanup spot in the batting order. Right away, the team showed its strength. The Braves won 9 of their first 10 games of the season. Warren Spahn, at age 36, went on to earn a 21-11 won-loss record. Lew Burdette won 17 games. Schoendienst batted .309, and Mathews .292, with 32 homers.

On September 23, 1957, Milwaukee needed to beat St. Louis to win the National League pennant. The game was long and close. In the 11th inning, it was tied, 2-2.

It was late, almost midnight, and players from both teams were tired. But when Henry Aaron stepped to the plate in the bottom of the inning, he knew that the pennant was on the line. He took one of Billy Moffett's pitches and sent it sailing over the centerfield fence.

Aaron barely had touched home when his teammates hoisted him on their shoulders and carried him off the field. It is still one of Aaron's greatest memories. Riding his peers off the field. Grinning like he'd just been named king of Wisconsin. And knowing that the Braves were N.L. champions once again.

Next came the World Series. Milwaukee's opponents were the New York Yankees, who had beaten the Dodgers in 1956 for the World Championship.

Whitey Ford beat the Braves and Warren Spahn, 3-1, in Game One. But in Game Two, a grim-faced, determined Lew Burdette tossed a 7-hitter and stopped the Yanks, 4-2.

New York's Tony Kubek, a native of Milwaukee, hit two home runs and scored three of his teammates as the Yanks trounced Milwaukee, 12-1, in Game Three. But Spahn came back to win the fourth game, 7-5, thanks to an alert play by Vernal "Nippy" Jones. Here's how it happened:

Jones was a seldom-used, backup first baseman for the Braves. He went to bat as a pinch-hitter in the bottom of the tenth inning.

Milwaukee had been ahead, 4-1, in the top of the ninth, but New York rallied to tie the game. When the Yankees went ahead, 5-4, in the top of the tenth, most of the Braves figured they'd blown that game for sure.

Jones was a surprise pinch-hitter. Even some of the Braves were shocked at Manager Fred Haney's choice, but it paid off. New York pitcher Tommy Byrne threw a pitch that umpire Hugie Donatelli called a ball. But Jones was hopping around on one foot—he said the ball hit his foot, and he should receive a walk.

Donatelli didn't believe him. Suddenly, Jones had an idea. He asked to see the ball. Sure enough, there was a black mark on the ball where it had hit Jones' polished shoe. Donatelli sent Jones to first, where he was promptly replaced by a pinch runner.

The Braves rallied from there, and Murray's two-run homer gave Milwaukee the win.

Burdette and Ford had a pitching battle in Game Five. Whitey held the Braves to 6 hits. Burdette allowed the Yanks 7, but Milwaukee scored one run and won, 1-0.

**1957
Warren Spahn becomes the first Braves pitcher to win the Cy Young Award, and Lew Burdette throws two straight World Series shutouts to spark the Braves to a World Championship over the Yanks.**

25

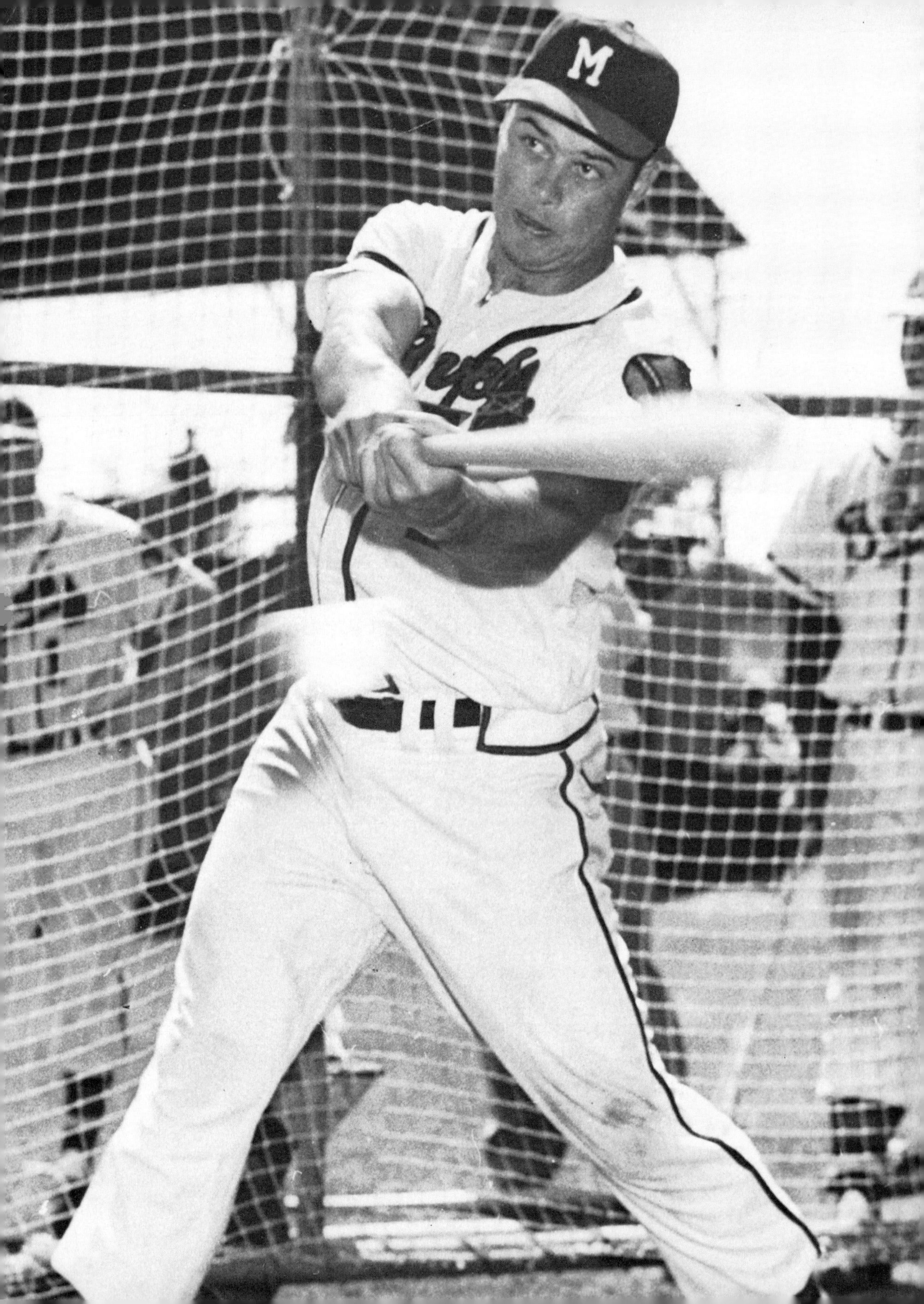
M

New York won the sixth game, 3-2. The Series came down to the final, seventh contest.

Haney wanted to start Spahn, since Burdette had received only two days' rest. But Spahn had been weakened by a virus, and Burdette got the nod.

On the mound for the Yankees was Don Larsen. One year and two days earlier, Larsen had pitched a perfect game for the Yankees in the 1956 World Series.

But it was Burdette's day in 1957. He shut out the powerful Yanks, 5-0. Lew had pitched two straight World Series shutouts, the first since legendary Christy Mathewson did so in 1905. Burdette had held the Yankees scoreless for 24 straight innings. He had won three games. And the Braves won the World Championship!

1958
The Braves go to the World Series again, but their loss to the Yankees triggers a club slump that will last for many years.

The Braves Move South To Atlanta

It looked as if Milwaukee would do it again in 1958. Again, the Braves won the pennant. Again, they faced the Yankees. Again, the Series was tied, three games each, going into the seventh game. Again, Burdette was the pitcher. Again, Larsen pitched for New York.

Souvenir vendors lined the streets of Milwaukee, just as they did in 1957. There were extra police on duty to handle the victory celebration, and mobile television and radio units stood by.

But there was no celebration in 1958. The Yankees won the deciding game, 6-2.

That 1958 World Series year was the last time the Milwaukee Braves won a National League pennant. No one really knows why Milwaukee slowly dropped out of contention, but Henry Aaron had a theory.

"We were fat, rich and spoiled," Aaron said later,

PHOTO
Ed Mathews warms up the wood in spring training, 1957. Eddie's eyes were on a World Series championship—and he got it.

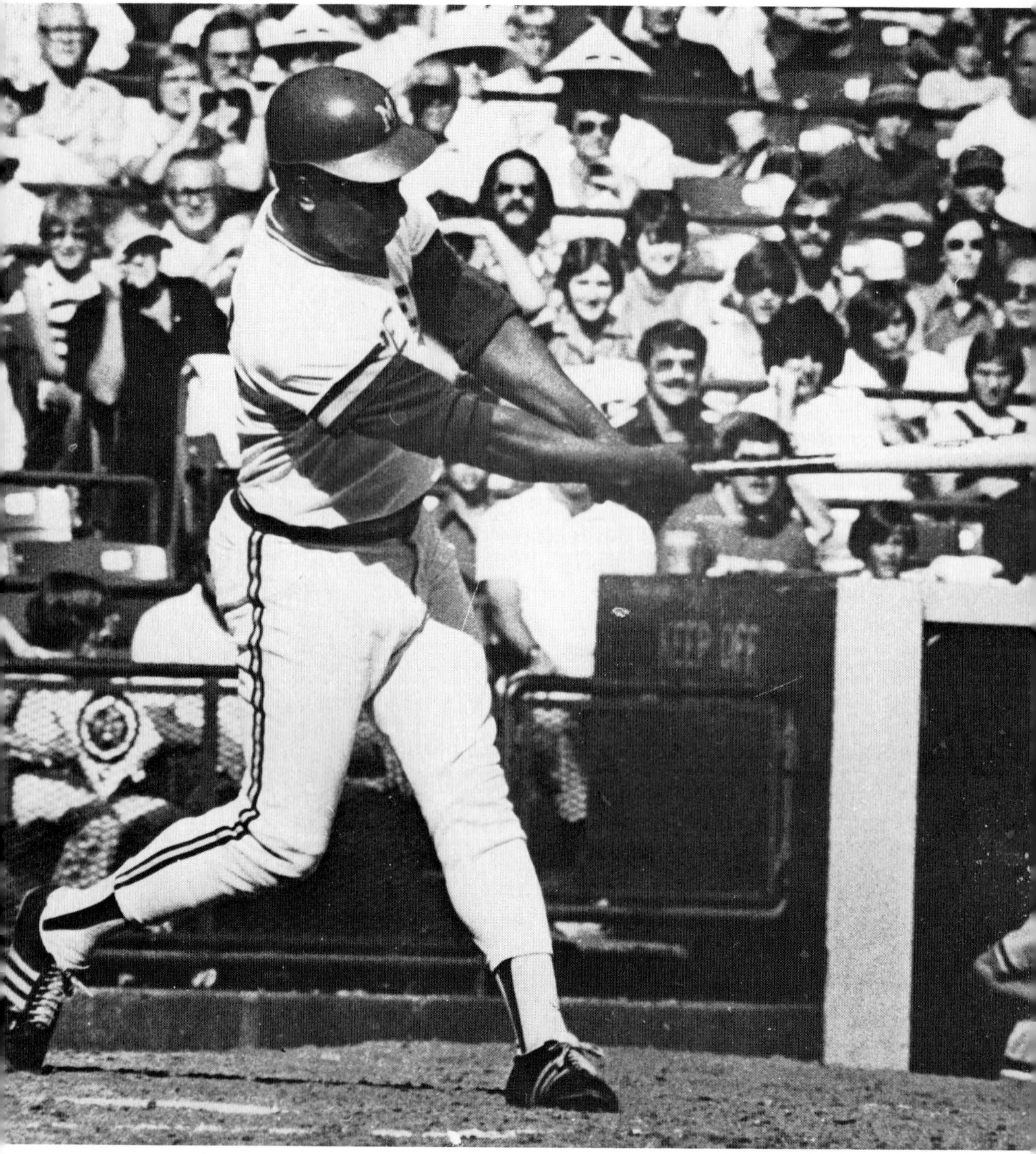
KEEP OFF

recalling the seasons after 1958. "And the fans were spoiled, too."

Milwaukee finished second in 1959 and 1960. The Braves dropped to fourth in 1961, fifth in 1962, sixth in 1963, and fifth in both 1964 and 1965.

By then, Milwaukee's fans had lost their enthusiasm for the team. From an all-time attendance record of 2,215,404 in 1957, the number of fans going to Braves' games fell to 555,584 in 1965. It was again time for a change. This time, the move was to Atlanta, Georgia.

Actually, the Braves' owner had first thought about moving the club to Atlanta as early as 1963. But Milwaukee wouldn't let go right away, and the case spent time in court before finally being settled. By the time the Braves actually moved to Atlanta for good, there was already a new stadium and thousands of fans waiting for them.

Attendance shot up again after the team moved to Georgia. In 1966, it rose by almost one million over the previous year, and it stayed over one million for five more years. But try as it did, the club couldn't win another pennant.

The Braves came close in 1969. Though they won the new Western Division of the National League, Atlanta lost the pennant playoff to the New York Mets, who would go on to win the World Series and become known as "The Amazing Mets."

In 1973, Atlanta had the best hitting team in history — the first club ever to have three players hit 40 or more home runs in one season. But that same year, Atlanta also had the worst pitching in the league, and the Braves finished second-to-last in their division.

In spite of the losing records, the Braves in recent

1966
The Braves move from Milwaukee to Atlanta—and attendance at home games skyrockets.

PHOTO
The final swing of home-run king Hank Aaron came in 1976. Hammerin' Hank ended up with 755 home runs in 23 years.

29

1969
With Manager Lumen Harris at the helm, the Braves win their first Division Championship, only to be edged out in the N.L. series by the "Amazin' Mets."

years have always given their fans some special moments to remember. One particular episode—you guessed it—involved Henry Aaron.

Bad Henry Shatters Ruth's Home Run Record

Every year, in spite of the Braves' sagging record, Aaron had been doing his thing. He'd always hit over or near the .300 mark. He'd play in 150 to 160 games. He'd go to bat nearly 600 times a year. He'd score at least 100 runs himself, and drive in another 100 or more.

And he'd keep hitting those home runs.

In 1971, at the age of 37, he hit 47 homers, his highest single-season total ever. Another year he hit 45 homers, and four times he hit 44—his uniform number. Each season, Aaron would send between 30 and 40 pitches into the bleachers.

Eventually, baseball followers began to realize that Aaron had a chance to break Babe Ruth's career home run record—the record everyone had thought was untouchable—714 homers.

Aaron didn't think about the record much. He actually didn't know a lot about Ruth. But by the time spring of 1973 rolled around, Henry Aaron had accumulated 673 round-trippers. Before he knew it, everyone, everywhere, wanted to ask about Ruth's record.

Not everyone was encouraging. Although he didn't tell anyone at first, Aaron was getting some mean hate mail from people who didn't want to see a black man break a white man's record. But as soon as Aaron admitted to getting those nasty letters, his real fans sent him notes of praise and encouragement that outnumbered the others, one thousand to one.

PHOTO
Braves ace Gene Garber posted a respectable 2.54 ERA during the '86 campaign.

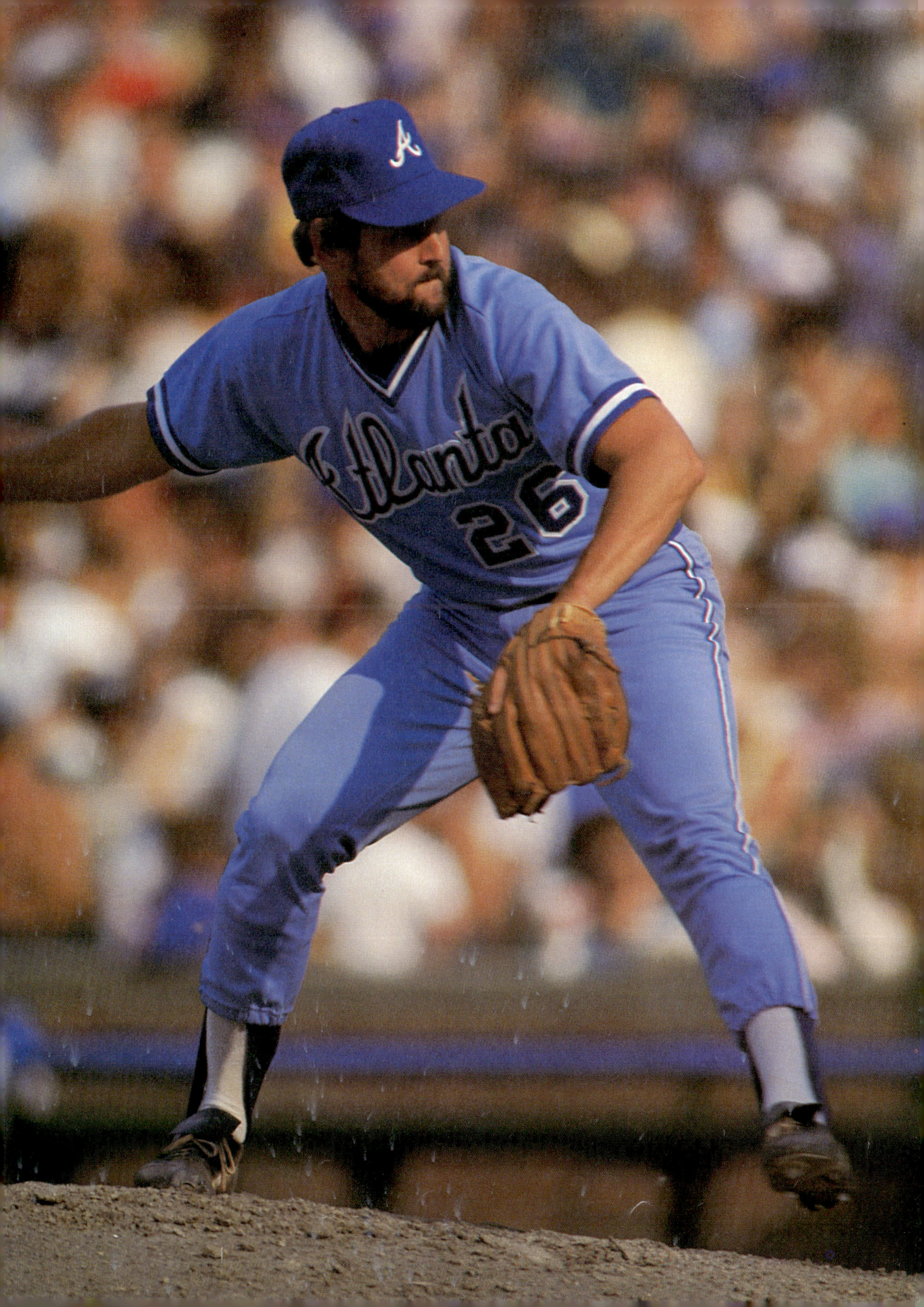
A
26

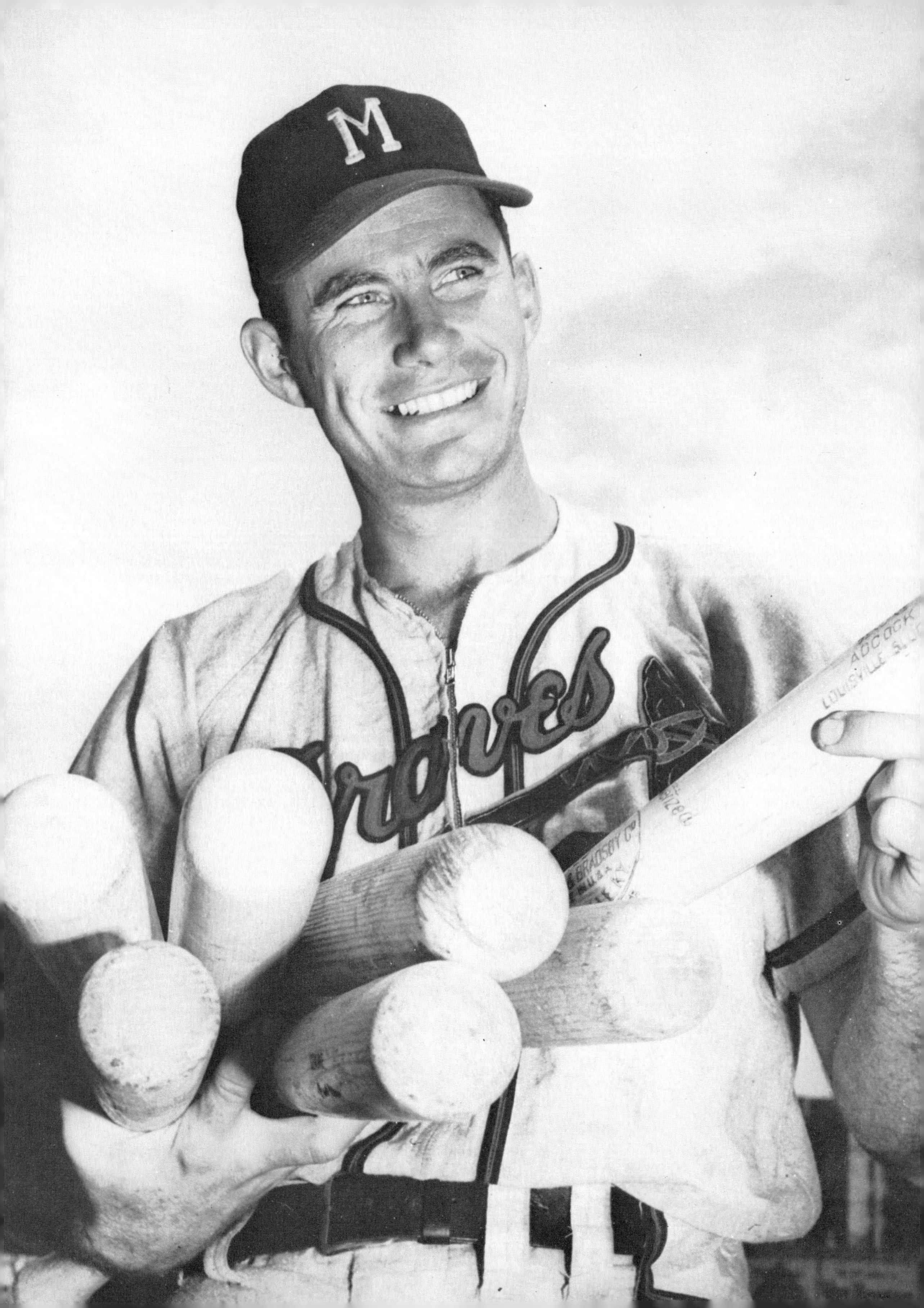

Aaron hit 40 home runs in 1973. That raised his total to 713, one shy of Ruth's record. Suspense at the end of the season was excruciating. Home run number 713 was exciting — and, from then on, any pitch that Henry *didn't* turn into a home run was disappointing.

All along, though, Aaron kept calm. He knew he'd be back next year. He knew there was no hurry. Besides, he was more interested in helping his team win than in setting records.

The record came, of course. Aaron tied Ruth's record with homer number 714 early in the 1974 season. Then, on April 8, 1974, the Braves hosted the Los Angeles Dodgers in Atlanta Stadium.

Hard-throwing lefty Al Donning was on the mound for the Dodgers. You could sense a strange excitement in the air.

Aaron came to bat for the second time in the game in the fourth inning. He went through his usual routine, as he had done for 20 years in the major leagues.

He waited in the on-deck circle, watching Downing pitch. "Hitting is mostly thinking," Aaron once said, and he had a memory bank in his mind that filed away the pitcher's pitches. He knew what Downing could do.

Aaron handed his extra bat to the batboy. No flashy swinging of two bats or tossing of one aside. He walked calmly toward the plate and slipped into the batter's box. He eyed Downing and took several slow, careful practice swings. Aaron breathed deeply.

"Aaron catches up on his sleep when he's batting," some pitchers claimed. But he was merely concentrating, relaxing, getting ready for that pitch. He knew the strike zone down to the millimeter, and he had the patience to wait for his pitch.

1969
Braves fans select an all-time Braves lineup, including Joe Adcock, Red Schoendienst, Eddie Mathews, Walter Maranville, Hugh Duffy, Filipe Alou, Hank Aaron, Del Crandell Lew Burdette and Warren Spahn.

PHOTO
Fence buster. On July 31, 1954, Milwaukee first baseman Billy Joe Adcock belted four home runs and a double for a total of 18 bases in a single game, a new major-league record.

1973
The Braves boast the first lineup in modern baseball history to have three players hit 40 or more homers in a single season.

The pitch came. It seemed to be almost past him when, suddenly, Aaron's body came alive. Those huge wrists snapped his 33-ounce bat around in a wooden blur. The ball collided with the fat part of the bat and went flying back over the fielders' heads. It was caught all right, by relief pitcher Tom House, who was in the Atlanta bullpen watching the action. It was home run number 715, and Henry Aaron was crowned baseball's new Sultan of Swat.

Though Hank Aaron wore the Braves uniform, his exploits were cherished and appreciated by baseball fans in every city and town in America. Through three different decades, his records and accomplishments inspired the nation. Today, the highlights of his long and storied career are still relived each day for hundreds of visitors at the Baseball Hall of Fame.

The Ted Turner Years

In 1976, a brash young tycoon by the name of Ted Turner purchased the team. Turner was many things: A hard-nosed business man . . . a self made millionaire . . . a world-class yacht racer . . . a pioneer in the development of the cable television industry . . . and, of course, a die-hard baseball fan.

"I bought a big-league team because I love the game–simple as that," explained Turner. "I can't say that it will turn out to be a great business decision, but I *can* say it should certainly be a lot of fun running the team."

Did Turner say "running" the team? "Hmmm," thought the Atlanta fans. "It sounds as if Mr. Turner intends to be one of those pesky owners who pokes his nose into every little decision that the General Man-

PHOTO
Ken Oberkfell took over at the Braves' hot corner when Bob Horner was switched to first. (1985)

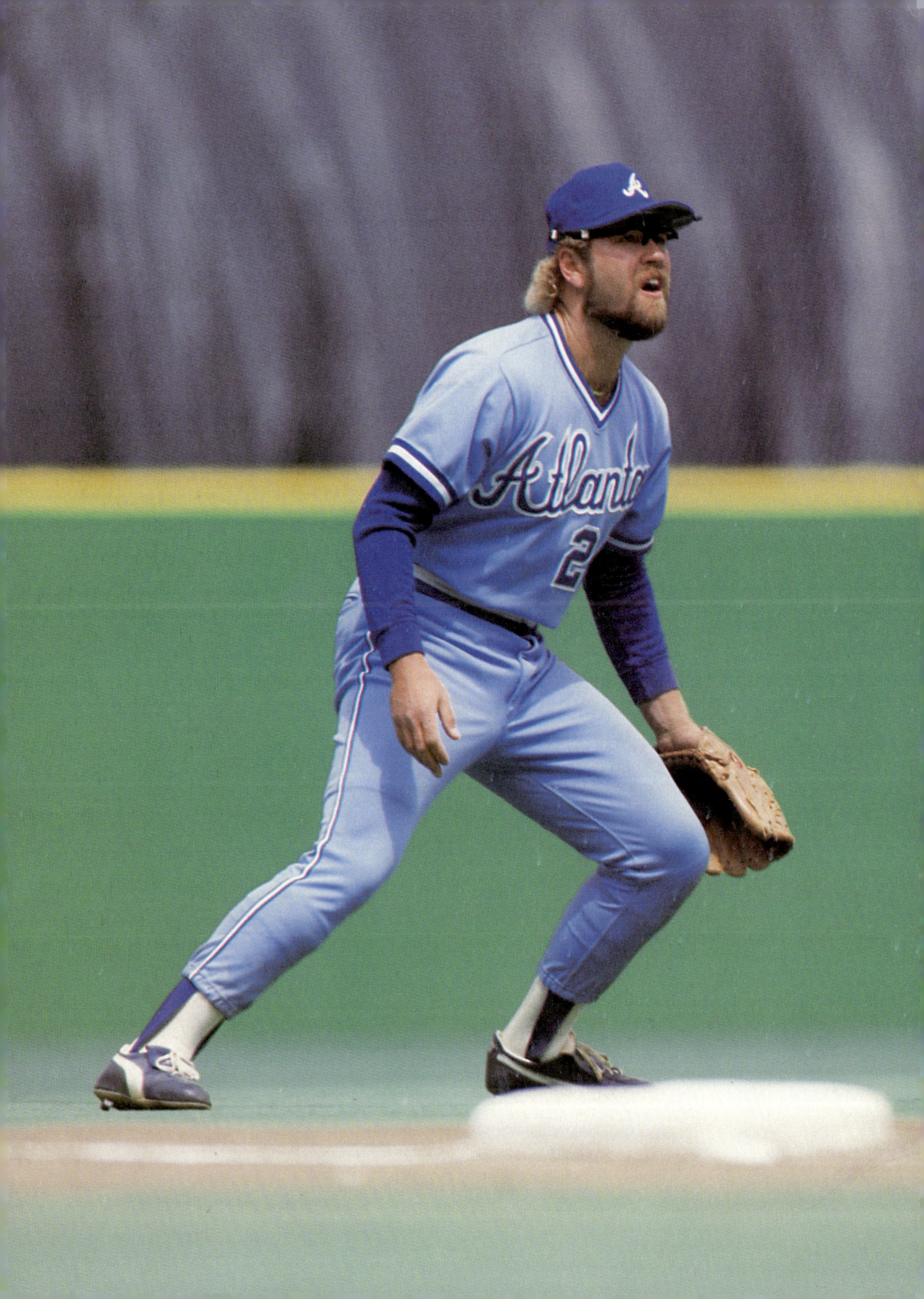
Atlanta

April 8, 1974 "Hammerin' Hank" Aaron hits homer number 715 to break Babe Ruth's all-time career home run record.

ager, field manager and coaches are supposed to make."

Sure enough. Over the next decade, it often seemed as if Ted Turner was competing with the Yankees' George Steinbrenner for the official title of the Most Meddlesome Owner. No decision was too small for Ted to be involved in. (In 1986 he would finally admit, "I was never really qualified to make some of the decisions I've made for the team over the years.")

Meanwhile, Braves fans endured nine losing seasons in Turner's first 12 campaigns. Even so, those years were loaded with exciting highlights, especially during the early 1980's. And, thanks to Ted Turner, the fans in Atlanta also had a front-row seat for some of the decade's most unusual situations and predicaments.

Take the Braves' 1980 season, for example. When ace sportswriter Ken Picking attempted to describe the events of that campaign for the *Official Baseball Guide*, he could only ask:

"What kind of team would lose 16 of 18 games to (last-place) Cincinnati and win 11 of 12 from (first-place) Pittsburgh?

"What kind of team would demote one of baseball's top power hitters (third baseman Bob Horner) to the minors and bench (Gary Matthews) its only 1979 All-Star?

"What kind of team would stop using a pair of million-dollar relievers (Gene Garber and Al Hrabosky) and turn to one (Rick Camp) coming off elbow surgery as its stopper?

"What kind of a team would take a catcher (Dale Murphy) and make him a center fielder?

"What kind? To the surprise of few Georgians, who

have become accustomed to their team's antics the last decade, it was the Atlanta Braves who did all those wild and crazy things and finished 81-80, their best record since 1974. It was the first team owned by Ted Turner that did not finish sixth in the National League West."

The very next year — 1981 — the Braves' front office launched the season with an upbeat promotional theme: "This Could be the Year." It wasn't. Instead, the Braves went a disappointing 50-56, finishing 15 games behind Cincinnati.

When Turner reacted by firing Manager Bobby Cox (apparently for no specific reason), the Atlanta reporters wanted to know why. "Sometimes in baseball you're supposed to make a change, just for the sake of making a change," explained Turner, leaving everyone including the players even more confused.

Wait, there's more. During the off-season, the Braves front office failed to make any trades. They failed to sign Reggie Jackson, the only free-agent they pursued. They failed to bring up any good farm team talent to improve their two weakest positions — shortstop and starting pitcher. In fact, their only success was in coaxing Joe Torre (the former catcher for the Braves from 1960-68) to sign on as the club's new manager. Oddly enough, signing Torre was the only change necessary.

**1976
Millionaire
Ted Turner purchases the Braves.**

Torre's Prediction Comes True In '82

When Joe showed up at spring training in mid-February of 1982, the reporters clustered around him. They knew that Torre was inheriting a discouraged, downtrodden team.

"What can you possibly promise these guys, Joe?"

37

1982
Braves set modern big-league record by winning their first thirteen games. (The amazing feat will be matched by the Milwaukee Brewers in 1987.)

was the first question on everyone's mind.

"I'll promise them nothing," snapped Joe. "I'll just tell the truth. I'll tell them that I truly believe the Braves have the talent to win the division championship this year, *if* these players want it bad enough."

Joe's prediction was laughable to some, but it was music to the ears of the Atlanta players. For a dozen years, the Braves had been the league goats at season's end. They had been teased and taunted, humbled and humiliated, beaten and belittled. Now, with Joe Torre's vote of confidence ringing in their ears, the Braves decided it was time to turn the tables. It was time, in other words, to win the championship.

They did it by opening the season with a scintillating 13-game win streak!

They did it by calling on gray-haired Phil Niekro, their 43-year-old knuckleball pitcher, for 17 wins including two straight shutouts!

They did it by rotating 12 different pitchers into the starting position throughout the season!

They did it by poking more home runs than any other team in the league! Centerfielder Dale Murphy had 36; third baseman Bob Horner had 32; first baseman Chris Chambliss had 20; and rightfielder Claudell Washington had 16.

They did it with thievery (a team record for stolen bases), and with double plays (shortstop Raphael Ramirez and second baseman Glenn Hubbard combined to lead the league in doubles.)

"Most of all," said rifle-armed relief pitcher Steve Bedrosian, "we did it with great coaching. I can't say enough about (pitching coaches) Rube Walker and Bob Gibson . . . and, of course, Joe Torre. These guys had

**PHOTO
Braves outfielder Claudell Washington in a rare bunt attempt.**

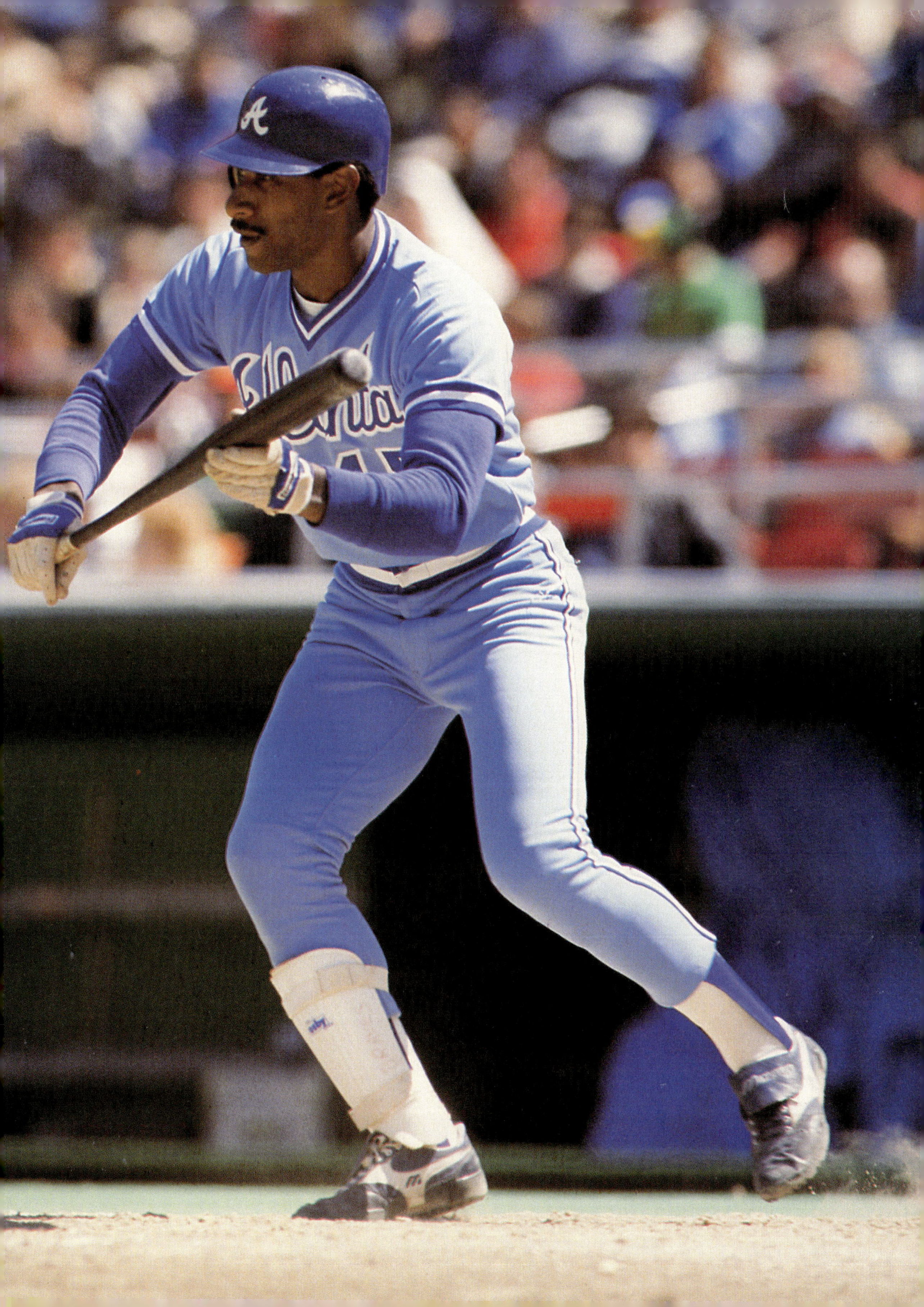

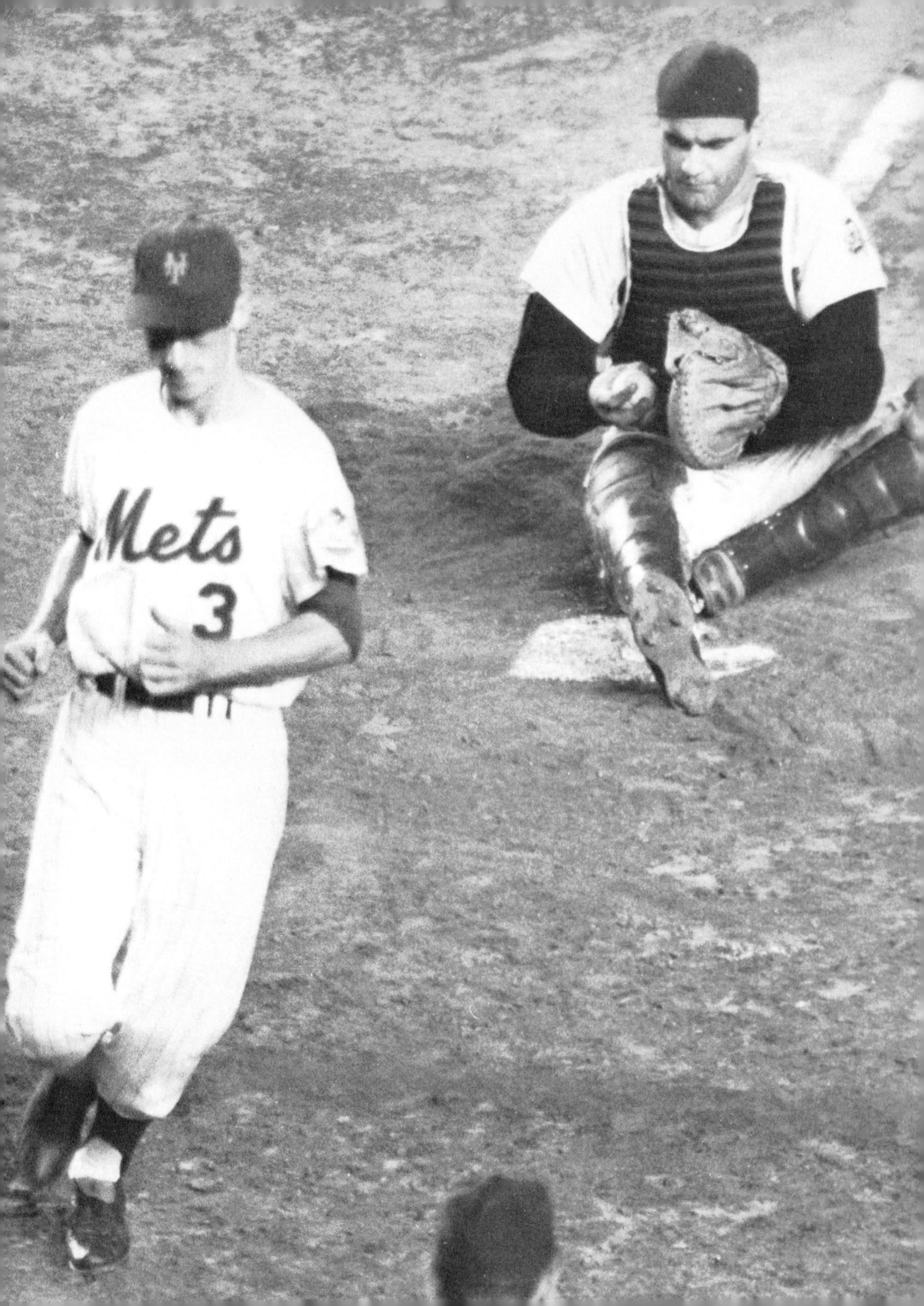

Mets
3

their heads in the ball game on every pitch and every play. Many times they were able to give us the slight edge because of a heads-up substitution or some special little strategy."

Though Torre's boys were swept by the Orioles in the Championship Series, that could not block the joy that gushed through the streets of Atlanta in 1982. After all, the last time the Braves fans had tasted a championship was in 1969 when the club had won the division title. The longer the wait, the sweeter the feeling.

1982
Joe Torre leads Braves to Division Championship in his first season as skipper.

World Series Task Force Fizzles

Winning the division championship in his very first year as manager of the Braves was the best thing that ever happened to Joe Torre. As things turned out, however, it was also the worst.

"The problem was, it got people's mouths watering for what's next," said Joe, meaning that the Atlanta fans were thinking nothing but "World Series" when 1983 rolled around. Even the mayor got in the act by forming a special "World Series Task Force" to prepare the city for the celebrations and pageantry that would surely accompany a World Championship playoff for Atlanta.

Hopes climbed higher and higher as the Braves held on to first place through most of the summer. Then disaster struck on August 15 when team leader Bob Horner—Mr. Inspiration—was benched for the rest of the year with a broken wrist.

Without Horner's spirit and clout, the offense sputtered and stalled. By September 1, the Braves were out of the pennant race. Atlanta's World Series Task Force closed up shop. More than a few disappointed fans

PHOTO
Braves catcher Joe Torre sits on the plate after Bud Harrelson scored in 1966 action. Torre, who hated to lose, later signed on as manager for the Braves.

1983
Dale Murphy erupts for a club record 131 runs in a single season.

blamed the team's woes on — yup — Joe Torre.

The following season — 1984 — found the Braves' skipper in even more hot water. This time it was a torrent of injuries that doused Torre's pennant hopes. It began the very first week of the season when pitcher Terry Forster, fielder Terry Harper and second baseman Randy Johnson were all knocked out of the starting lineup. Nearly 50 additional injuries followed during the summer months. A dozen key players, including big Bob Horner (again!) were placed on the disabled list, forcing poor Joe Torre to experiment with more than 100 different lineups.

Meanwhile, owner Ted Turner had ordered the executives of his cable "superstation" to regularly broadcast Braves games to his television viewers throughout the nation. Turner hoped that his team would attract fans in every American city, thereby becoming what he called "America's Team." If anything, however, the national spotlight just put more pressure on Torre and his troops.

Despite all the distractions, injuries and confusion, Torre was still able to lead the gimpy '84 Braves to an 80-82 record, good enough for a second-place finish in the National League West . . . but not quite good to save Torre from the unemployment line. After the season, Turner fired Joe and replaced him with Eddie Haas, a 20-year veteran of Atlanta's farm system.

Haas did his best, but the players complained that he was too nice — too willing to give in and let the players themselves run things.

By the end of August, 1985, the Braves had slipped to a 50-71 record. At that point, an irate Ted Turner stepped in, fired Haas and promoted coach Bobby

PHOTO
The Braves paid plenty to keep Dale Murphy on the roster for the rest of the 1980's.

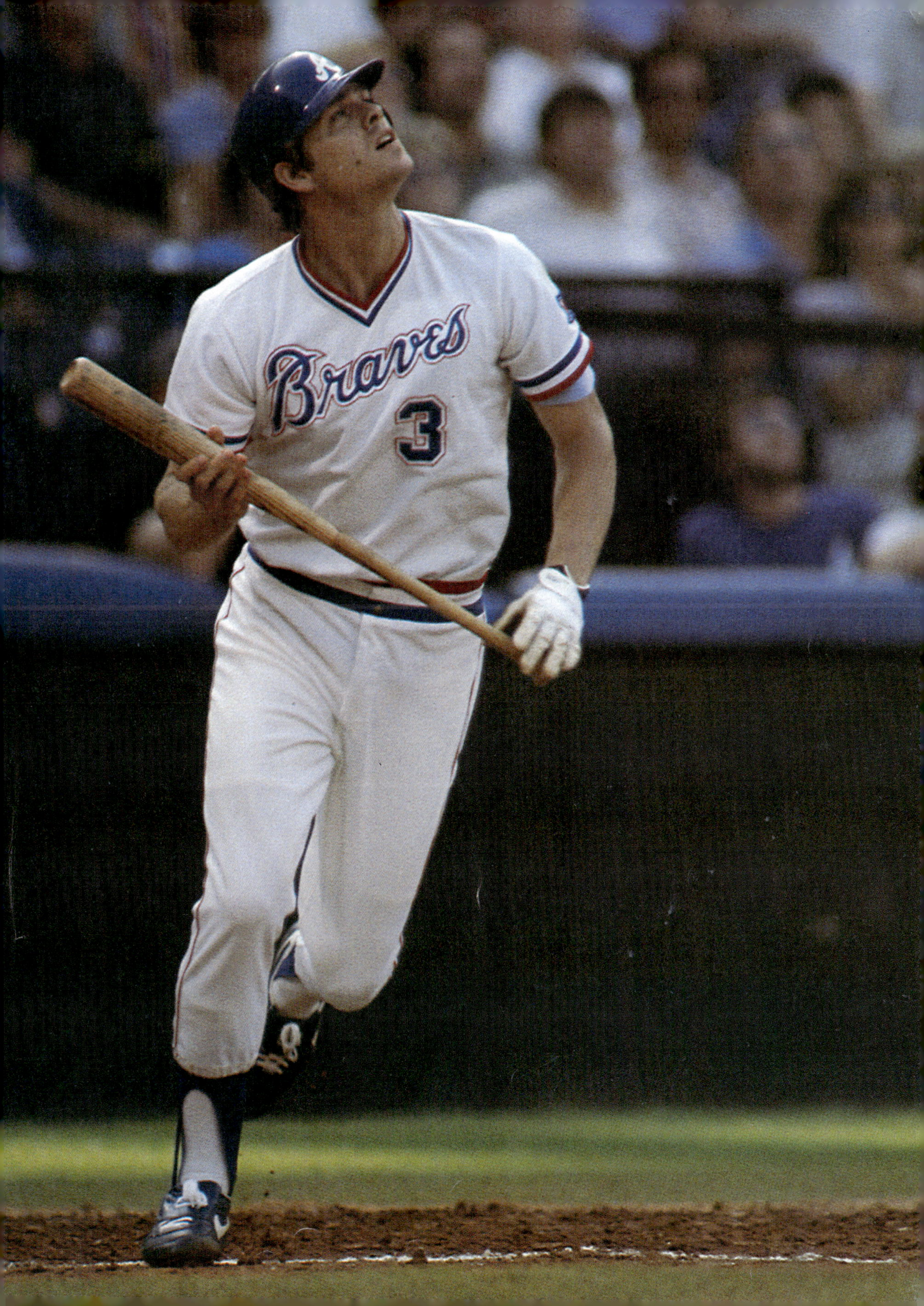
Braves
3

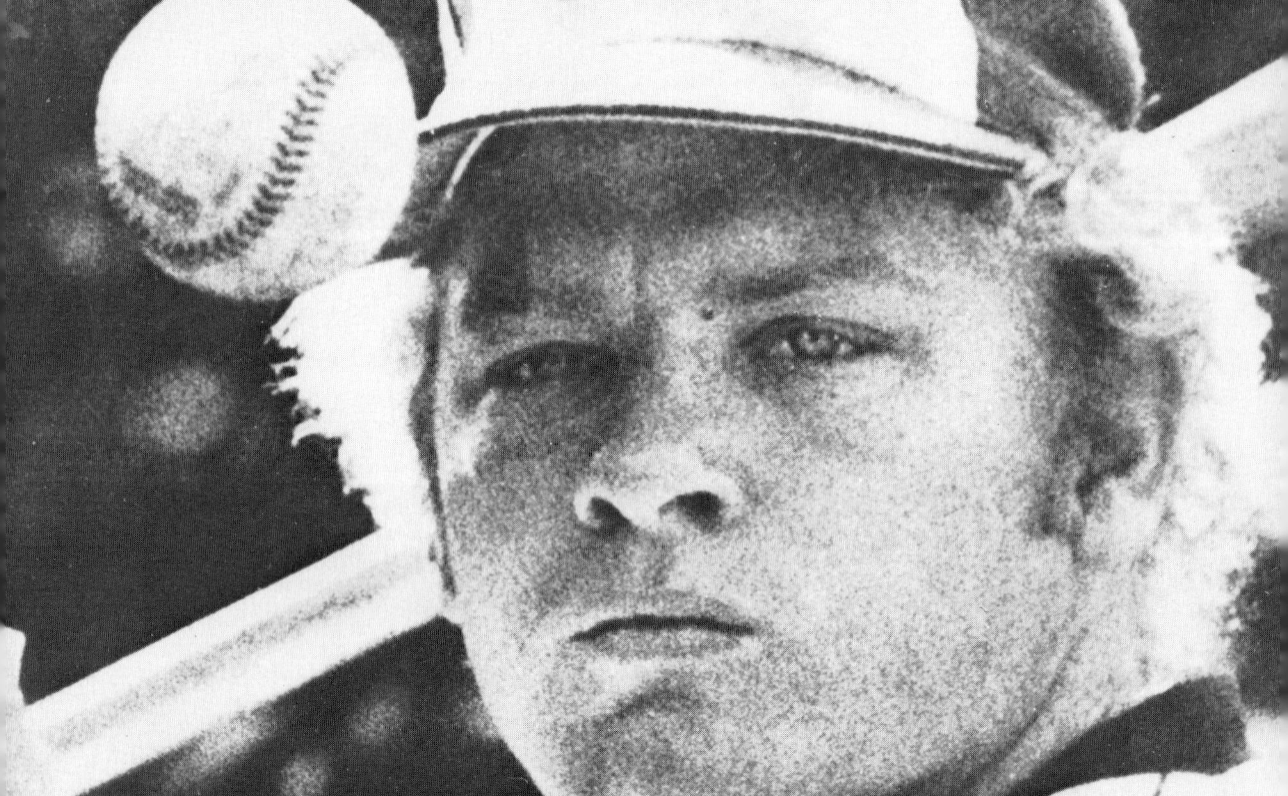

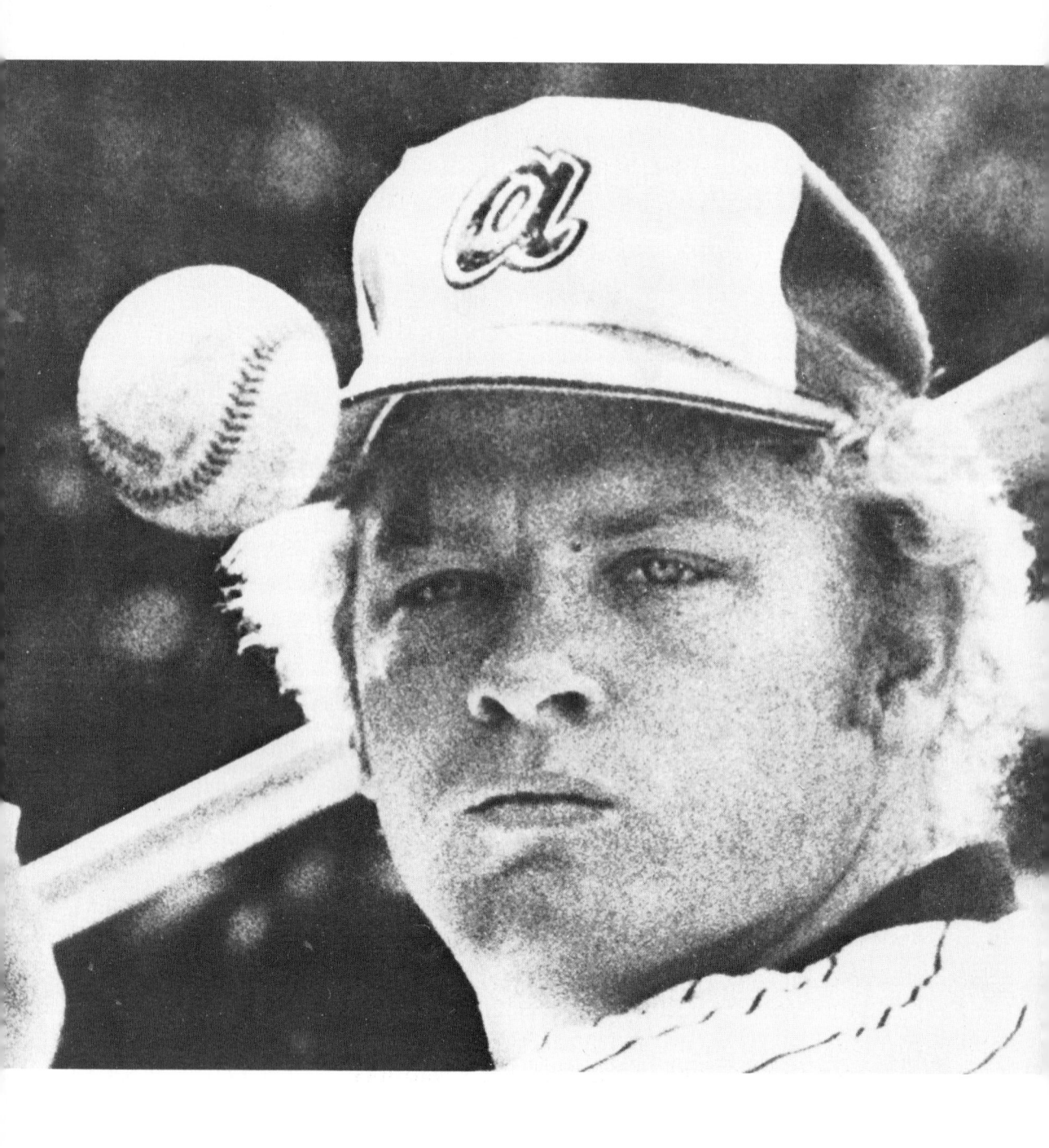

Wine to manager. Presto! The inspired Braves reeled off five straight victories, but it was too little too late. Sadly, the Braves would finish the '85 season in (gulp) fifth-place. Even sadder, there were very few Atlanta fans in the stands to support them.

"The Braves' home attendance (in '85) was surpassed by every N.L. club except for Houston, Pittsburgh and San Francisco, and only the Astros were less popular on the road," reported Gerry Fraley in the *Official Baseball Guide.* "In addition, ratings for Braves games on Owner Ted Turner's cable superstation were down. Apparently 'America's Team' loses its national appeal when it doesn't win."

**1986
Chuck Tanner takes over as skipper.**

Bright New Stars On The Horizon

In 1986, Ted Turner announced that he would remove himself from the daily operation of the team and allow General Manager Bobby Cox and new Field Manager Chuck Tanner to make most of the decisions. It was a refreshing change for the entire organization.

Though the '86 club finished with a losing record, Turner himself complimented Cox and Tanner and admitted, "They made a lot of moves that I never had the courage to make. Sure, we all would've liked to have done better in '86, but the moves we made will be positive for us in 1987, '88 and beyond. I think we got something to work with for the future."

For starters, as the beginning of the 1987 season loomed closer, the Braves were working overtime to sign free agents Doyle Alexander, Bob Horner, David Palmer, Gene Garber, Ted Simmons and Dale Murphy. The cost to Ted Turner for these six contracts

**PHOTO
One of the top sluggers in the league, Bob Horner was named "Mr. Inspiration" by his Braves teammates. (1982)**

1987
The Braves head into the season with one of the oldest and highest-paid lineups in baseball.

alone? Approximately $8-million!

"Don't get the wrong idea, though," cautioned G.M. Bobby Cox. "We're not going to try to buy a pennant by chasing every big name who becomes a free agent. We're going to build this team from within. We've been watching the young kids in our farm system, and we think they're coming along just fine. There are definitely some bright new stars on the horizon."

Can you hear it in the voice of Bobby Cox? It's the positive sound of optimism coming through, loud and clear. Sure, the Braves have fallen on hard times over the past few years. And yes, they still have plenty of obstacles left to hurdle. But the oldest professional baseball club is not about to throw in the towel.

The Braves have won the World Series in Boston.

The Braves have won it it Milwaukee.

Now, it's Atlanta's turn.

PHOTO
Rafael Ramirez in another theft attempt against the Cubbies.

Atlanta Braves /
796.3 ROT   11011
Rothaus, James.
         ST. ANDREW MEDIA CENTER